# *Water my Soul*

## Reflections in Poetry

Arwa Qutbuddin

Illustrations by Fatema Qutbuddin

First published in 2018 by

**Becomeshakespeare.com**

Wordit Content Design & Editing Services Pvt. Ltd.
Unit - 26, Building A -1, Nr Wadala RTO,
Wadala (East), Mumbai 400037, India
T: +91 8080226699

Wordit Art Fund helps deserving authors publish their work by providing monetary support. To apply for funding,
please visit us at
www.BecomeShakespeare.com

Copyrights © 2018, Arwa Qutbuddin

All rights reserved. Any unauthorized reprint or use of this material is prohibited. No part of this book may be reproduced or transmitted in any form or by any means, electronic or mechanical, including photocopying, recording, or by any information storage and retrieval system without express written permission from the author/publisher.

Please do not participate in or encourage piracy of copyrighted materials in violation of the author's rights. Purchase only authorized editions.

ISBN-9789388081214

# *Gratitude*

*To feel grateful is a blessing.*

Where do I begin? As I see more and more clearly the invisible hand of Grace holding and guiding me through this mysterious journey called life, I feel more and more blessed and humbled.

My poetry comes from all who have touched my life -- in big ways and small. To all of them I am grateful.

To Syedna Mohammed Burhanuddin, I offer my sincere devotion and love. He gave me the gift of light.

To my parents, *Bawaisab* and *Busaab*, who gave me the gift of sincerity, and planted in me the seeds of faith and love, I owe my deepest gratitude. My (late) father, Syedna Khuzaima Qutbuddin, spiritual leader of the Bohra Community, personified the ideals of truth, courage, compassion, and goodness; he made me wish wholeheartedly that I embrace and become them. It is now my brother Syedna Taher Fakhruddin, who has taken his place as our spiritual leader, and who exemplifies fearlessness and conviction in the path of virtue and righteousness; I seek and cherish his blessings. My mother, Sakina, a woman of true substance with utmost trust in God, a sharp intellect and a cheerful child-like heart models for me the beauty of strength and softness. Both my parents showed me what it means for gold to be purified through fire. They nurtured within me the soulfulness which makes me a poet, a philosopher, a lover of wisdom, a seeker of truth.

To my five beautiful children who came through me as blessings of the Almighty: Sakina, Mohammed, Taher, Mustafa, Murtaza (papa), each one, the apple of my eye. They gave birth to the mother in me; the deep unconditional love that a mother is blessed to feel for her children, the priceless memories which warm my heart and make it glow are their gift to me and so much of it finds its way into my poetry. To each one of them I want to say: *Beta*, may the light of love within you shine and lead you to true faith.

To my *jaan*, my best friend, who rekindled my inner flame when it had all but died: May your life be filled with light, love, beauty, peace and joy.

To my dearest brothers: Abdeali, Husain, Aziz, and my dearest sisters: Tahera, Saifiyah, Tayyebah and Fatema who showered me with love and affection, warmth and care in my childhood and youth and continue to do so. My sister-in-law Insiya, a kind and caring friend. *Jazakumullaho khairan kaseeran.*

To all my nieces and nephews, each one of you is a bundle of joy. Zahra, a blooming rose, a budding poet.

To my dear friend Shivani who is full of love and shares it so generously with me. It has been her dream to get my poems published.

To my dear friends, Partho, Shaan, Suhail, Pesi, Babu, Sammy, Vinit, Fiona, Beth, Chris, Nadia, Sivan, Archana,

Zareena, Ubai, Anup and many others who stood by me and helped me see the beauty within 'Good friends are like stars, you don't always see them but you know they are there.'

To my dear community members who care for me and pray for me with love. May you all be blessed.

To my students who bring me joy; my teachers who encourage me, guide me, nurture me with kindness and patience.

To the many who have played a part, large or small, in my journey. Some have given me love, some have given me lessons, some have stayed with me through thick and thin, some have come and left, to all of them I offer thanks.

To the sun, the moon, the stars, the sky. To the earth, the oceans, the forests, the deserts, the mountains, the rivers, and the wind…Where do I end?

# Contents

| | |
|---|---|
| **Foreword** | **11** |
| **Poet's Note** | **15** |
| | |
| **Categories of Poems** | |
| **Soulful** | **21** |
| Musings | 23 |
| Sacred Space | 25 |
| Sometimes | 27 |
| Fruitful Rage | 29 |
| Dark Spaces | 30 |
| Melting | 32 |
| Seeking | 34 |
| Breakthrough | 35 |
| Blue Horizon | 37 |
| Becoming | 38 |
| Deep Dive | 40 |
| Life-strokes | 41 |
| Carry On | 42 |
| Fragile | 44 |
| Life Goes On | 46 |
| Paradox | 47 |
| The River Story | 49 |

| | |
|---|---:|
| Remembrance | 50 |
| Elusive | 51 |
| Topsy-Turvy | 53 |
| Tie-in | 55 |
| Note from Soul to my Heart | 56 |
| | |
| **Love** | **59** |
| Ever-lasting | 61 |
| Give it Time | 62 |
| Moments Live On | 63 |
| Togetherness | 65 |
| Story of Heartbreak | 67 |
| Beyond a Crescent | 70 |
| Wholeness | 71 |
| It's All There Is | 72 |
| To My Child | 73 |
| Broken Wings | 74 |
| Sakina's Portrait | 75 |
| Wish Fulfilled | 77 |
| Loved and Lost | 79 |
| Could It Be | 80 |
| | |
| **Nature** | **81** |
| Lie. Breathe. Bliss. | 83 |
| Walk in Matheran | 84 |
| Symphony | 86 |
| Play | 87 |
| Rider | 89 |

| | |
|---|---|
| Home | 90 |
| Peeling | 92 |
| Tree Talk | 94 |
| Virgin Eyes | 96 |
| Coming Back to Myself | 98 |
| Dream-catcher | 99 |
| Slice of Orange Moon | 101 |
| Soaked | 103 |
| Ripe Corn and Snow | 104 |
| Immersed | 105 |
| Journey | 106 |
| An Affair to Remember | 107 |

| | |
|---|---|
| **Life** | **111** |
| What's the Question | 113 |
| Hawk | 115 |
| Free-Fall | 116 |
| Piercings | 118 |
| Mindful Emptiness | 121 |
| Rainbow in the Puddle | 122 |
| My Father | 124 |
| Long Time Ago | 125 |
| Useful Reminders | 126 |
| Invisible Tattoos | 128 |
| Paint | 130 |
| Wholesome Existence | 131 |
| Joy of Work | 133 |
| Insatiable | 134 |

| | |
|---|---|
| Abuse | 135 |
| A Woman | 136 |
| It Simply Is | 137 |
| Fantasy | 138 |
| Flow | 140 |
| In His Shoes | 142 |
| Spoonful of Indifference | 143 |
| Cry No More | 144 |
| Wonder | 145 |
| Caving In | 147 |
| Shine I Will | 149 |
| From Rage to Redemption | 151 |
| Silver in Grey | 152 |
| Innocence Lost | 153 |
| Break Free | 155 |
| These Days | 157 |
| Holding On | 160 |

**Short Poems**     **161**

# *Foreword*

In our modern times, words are often brutally cut short to convey a message rapidly, with just a few words, a tweet. Language has become limited by the need for quick practicality, expressed with an emoji or uncertain ideas; it has become superficial, shallow, and gross. As if a strange paradox, despite the constant growth in means of communication, mainly thanks to the development of cyber networks, everyone connects with everyone else, through what seems to have become lesser and lesser meaningful relationships. Evidently, this affects not only the way we express ourselves, but also the way we think, the way we view the world around us, and ultimately, the way we know ourselves.

But not all is lost to this tendency of the exclusive materialistic viewpoint, the monster of modern life. As long as there exist philosophers and artists, lovers of Truth, Beauty, Justice and Goodness, there is hope; there shall remain a way to renew and arise from the ashes. In today's modern world, drowned under the weight of perhaps too many words, their voice is even more essential; they must be expressed firmly. We need to pay attention to them, today more than ever before, as they carry some keys for us, to open a chest of the most valuable treasure of all; a door to our inner world, the possibility to know ourselves, and the world around us, with new eyes and refreshed wonder.

Poetry has always seemed to me a kind of mysterious art. It is not merely a play of words, but an intimate message from the writer's inner world, sometimes distilled with only very few words. It maneuvers through a constant movement between the inner and the outer, revealing and yet hiding at the same time, sometimes stating something directly, sometimes indirectly, inviting the reader to explore over and over again. Sometimes, in the most harmonious way, with perfect rhyme and rhythm, a beautiful message is shared. Sometimes, the simplicity of the expression leaves a mark of incredible depth. Poetry, as with any real art form, expresses the richness of life, not only in quantity, but with quality as well, a refreshing inspiration of beauty and vitality. Today, maybe more than ever before, the spirit of a new poetry, new art, and renewed philosophy is needed. There is a need to direct our attention back to our inner world, so brutally neglected, but so vitally important.

I praise this compilation of beautiful poems by Arwa, that touches my heart, and feel a humble pride in writing this foreword. In her poems, one finds the yearning of a philosopher; love, devotion, pain, sadness, joy and faith… all come together as a reflection of her inner world, that she willingly and bravely shares with us. I find her poems full of life, reflections worthy to be absorbed quietly.

Yaron Barzilay
Director, New Acropolis India

*To Amma*
*the apple of my father's eye*

# Poet's Note

*"Bits of eternity*
*Lie scattered*
*Within this transience*
*And it is we*
*The people of the soul*
*Who have come to reclaim them"*

This collection of poems is called *Water My Soul*. Watering is a form of nurturing; which results in growth. The awakening of my soul, the unfurling of the petals of my being, the letting go of how things must be through a graceful acceptance of what is; a humbling realization of the laws of creation along with a deepening in the trust of 'oneness', there is a yearning in me for all the above and my search has been fuelled by life's longing to evolve and truly live. It is through my poetry that I sometimes, in rare moments of absolute peace and surrender, touch something elusive and mysterious, yet as authentic and real as the marrow in my bones. Once that subtle sense of near-divinity has been experienced the heart will relentlessly seek it over and over again and will not rest until it finds it, even though it means going through inner churning and grinding, and shedding layers that seem to be holding all parts of me together like my skin. Poetry tells me that it's okay to fall apart, to scatter, to shatter. It is an essential practice if one seeks to rise in consciousness and embrace both the dust and stardust. This journey of becoming testifies to the beauty of transformation in life through death.

I have divided the book into categories: Soulful, Life, Nature and Love. It is almost impossible to draw lines between these genres, but I have done so, if only to create a navigation chart for the reader who might be more drawn to one word over the other. In reality, what is life if not love? What is love if not soul? What is soul if not an extension of nature, of creation, of perfection?

I sometimes wonder where my poems come from and what are they about.

I go for a run in the Yeoor hills next to my home 3 times a week in the evenings when the sun is low and the breeze is cool. As I run, the vibrant lushness of the forest intoxicates me, inspires me. As nature comes alive, the world around me fades away, a deep silence awakens, and leads me to my heart, to my soul. Something shifts inside, a door opens. My spirit spreads its arms wide. Sometimes, in those strides, lines of poetry come to me as though carried upon the wind that blows through my hair. I marvel at the beauty and power of words; I bow my head even as my legs pick up speed. I feel a high, a poet's high when she is able to receive a gift from the skies and offer it as a poem on earth. It allows her to pen her heart and lay out on paper a few pieces of life-blood so that a passer-by might, perhaps, if the poet is lucky, be touched for a moment.

Change of scene. I also go to court regularly, to see my five kids. There is a room in Family Court called the Children's Complex where alienated kids and their non-custodial parents are given a space to meet, connect, break boundaries, and share togetherness. I see my blessed children, love flows from my eyes. They look at me and turn away, their tender hearts do not know any other way. How do I deal with this pain? I cry, I pray, I write poetry. I somehow find the strength to go on, to keep breathing, find a way to make sense of this nonsense that the world has come to.

My poems have been my pathway into the recesses of my heart, a trail into the maze of my mind, a dirt road into the crevices of my soul. Each poem that flows forth from my being helps me go deeper within. It's like an explorer's journey, and the compass that guides me is my longing to express what I feel, and my passion to discover what lies beneath it. 'Know thyself and you shall know thy God', isn't that what the wise men said? My poetry is, for me, worship, meditation, love, rage, solace, fury, catharsis, revenge, cleansing, succour, prayer, all in one and more.

Often I say to myself and my friends that words to me are like breath, they give me life. I do not know how I would live without them.

My poems are a cry for my deepest needs: worth, value, recognition, unconditional acceptance and love; a relentless plea to myself, to try and find these somewhere, somewhere outside, somewhere inside, anywhere. My poems are an expression of my pain, the pain of not feeling complete, the pain of feeling disconnected from the universe, from the divine. They are also an expression of the deep joy that comes to me in miracle moments when I feel whole, I feel safe, I feel enough, I feel God with me, by my side. My poems are a testimony to the efforts I have made in this life-time to seek answers that lead to profound questions, to find peace within, to find love in being, to find meaning in existence, to find a way to comprehend both the lowliness and the grandeur of reality, and to surrender to the mystery of what it means to be alive. My poems are my soul laid bare.

I started writing poems when I was a teenager, and many of my earlier poems reflect the hormonal roller coaster of youth. As I grew up, my realities changed, some changes brought joy, some brought pain. My craving for words continued to grow, and the content of my poems reflect the unfolding chapters of my story; the ephemeral transience of the overt as well as the stalwart quality of something deeper, something awe-inspiring. And now at the ripe age of forty I look back and see my life through the lens of my poetry. I cry. I smile. My poems are full of pain, sadness, trauma, and melancholia; they overflow with glimpses of courage, faith and joy. Every tear, every drop of joy has found itself into a poem. I see myself trying to make sense of my truth, striving to hold on to hope as I cope with the struggles that come my way, smiling to see how blessed I am. The more I write, the deeper I dive into the labyrinth of my inner world, and the wonders I discover there make me humble and proud all at once; glory comes with bowing; liberation comes with gratitude; the journey is never ending. One step at a time. One poem at a time. One word at a time. One breath at a time....

Love and Blessings,  
Arwa Qutbuddin

*Soulful*

# 1. Musings

Am I to whisper the secrets of the early-morning song
into the ears of the crescent moon as it fades into dawn

Will there be music in the movement of hands
that are raised in prayer to offer gratitude and seek grace

Why not kindle another's flame by fanning our own fire
so that our sparks of light can dance together to the flute
of promised friendships

The stardust that falls and settles on my eyelids when I sleep
brings with it visions of a boundless universe that carries
in its belly the sacred gift of life

The soft blades of grass that caress my feet
as I walk barefoot upon the earth,
awaken my sole to the touch of sweet being
that emanates from the soil of gentle wakefulness

The stains of coffee left in my cup after I have savoured
it spell themselves into names of people and places I have
long forgotten but yearn to recall

The date palms stand tall, like women who have learned
to rise from the ashes and find their way to higher truths,
here I come to stand tall beneath them now

The washed-away footprints on the beach tell stories of those who walked beside the ocean holding hands and let it wash away the salt of their tears with its own, see the touch of a smile upon this half erased foot print

What if the firefles find their way
into the spaces between my fingers and thoughts,
to lighten the heavy creases of entangled imaginations
that buzz in my mind until all is quiet, all is still

The window of my heart awaits an opening
to usher in the fresh aroma of wild flowers
strewn across the floor of lost dreams,
this forest within me breathes life into passers-by
and they leave imprints of their soul-talk
on barks of trees they walk past

Perhaps the moon will find its way back
into the open arms of the night sky.

## 2. Sacred Space

Deep within each one of us is a space
Solid and serene like the mountains
Graceful and vibrant like a river
Rooted and sturdy like a hundred year old oak tree
Vast in its magnitude like the open cloudless sky

Powerful and boundless like the ocean
Sharp in perception like a polished diamond
Soft like the petals of a red velvet rose
It is deep and still like the waters of a crystal clear lake
And light like the oxygen-rich air that we breathe
Full of love and life like a pregnant mother's womb

That space is the essence of who you are
Be still and silent and you shall find it
It is your being, make it your dwelling
Cherish every moment you spend there
Feel safe in its sanctity

Protected from the troubles and woes of this harsh world
Sheltered from the burden of doubts and fears
Shielded from regrets of the past
And worries of the future

That space knows only the present, only the here and now
It knows only to have complete faith
That all is well and always will be

It knows this absolute truth
That we are loved more than we will ever know
That the universe and all its forces
Are working for our good
That every moment that comes and goes
Brings us closer to eternity

That space is your stepping stone
To the kingdom of heaven
Find it
Be there
Stay.

## 3. Sometimes

Sometimes I feel myself in the soft sway of branches that make the leaves rustle as they let go and drift onto the ground to become the earth
I feel myself gently nudging my need for acceptance to loosen its hold, to fall away and dissolve into my ability to belong to myself and embrace my all

Sometimes I hear myself in the soft pitter patter of rain as the clouds break themselves into drops of liquid music, I let parts of me melt and float away to assimilate into the fluid rhythm of the universe

Sometimes I see myself in the waves
as they relentlessly work to find their way to the shore,
I see me momentarily touching the essence of creation in its elusive magnanimity

Sometimes I see myself in the colours of dusk that brush the sky and set it on fire, I see my zest for life ignite the flame of passion in my heart
and make it spill over into all the little and big things I do: like making a cup of tea, or giving someone a hand to hold, or saving my own sanity

Sometimes I see myself in the soft dark petals of a wild rose as it blossoms unseen in a quiet corner of the forest under a big oak tree

I see myself unfurl into the softness of my feminine grace,
as I bloom and blush under the quiet and alluring gaze of
the hazy blue summer sky

Sometimes I feel myself in the wind that gently whispers
your name into my ear and makes my spirit dance with
joy to the sweetness of breath and melody,
I find my name imprinted on the lines of your palms,
in the destiny that spells out our eternal togetherness

Sometimes I see myself in the smoke rising out of the
dying fire, I see myself striving to keep alive despite the
doom of dying dreams
I see myself in the burnt yet beautiful orange embers
that emblazon the charred landscape of my memories
and remind me of moments that make life worth living

Sometimes I see myself in the needles of sunlight
threading gold into the flowing fabric of water,
adorning it with a bridal light that shimmers on the
surface of the river as it flows effortlessly
into the opens arms of the sea
I see the shine of your soul-light
weaving into me the silk of heavenly union,
gliding with me to our heavenly abode.

## 4. *Fruitful Rage*

Melon yellow and musk, seeds burst forth
Like the passion of my rage
As it ruptures from my veins
Into a melting pot of wax and cranberries
I seethe in the fire that ignites my intestines
I burn in it unscathed, unapologetic
I am ready to become ash, only for the sake of honour

That flows like red hot lava, in my blood
I do not shout nor cry
I do not lose any of my senses
I have never been more aware
My consciousness has never been more awake
My insides have never felt more vitally aroused

A voice inside me loud and clear:
Harness this force
"Let it activate the parts of you that lull in dull apathy
And lie in mute resignation
Let it fuel your power
Let it drive you to the farthest limits of your potential"

The wax is smooth
The cranberries sweet
Anger is steaming my skin
Serenity soaks my soul
I simmer, I savour, I stay.

## 5. Dark Spaces

Distance between heart and mind,
Somehow, it's never crossed
Countless bridges built
To reach, to touch that non-ephemeral substance,
It lies still beyond realm of feeling and thought
But I fail

Sink deeper and deeper,
The ocean within me
A vast and shoreless space of soul,
I cannot find succour nor can I see my end,
For it goes on and on and on...
Life, fuelled by the need to seek

Stars, sun, sky, sand…something
Maybe the mystic moon,
Meaning for the seeker who yearns
To know, yet blinded by my faithlessness

I falter, trip, stumble, fall a million
Yes a million times; the law of gravity
Will not let me rise into the sky
I cry, oh how I cry!
The waves are high, salt and fury
Fill my mouth and ears; I think, I feel, I know
It will subside; Dark spaces
Within me, a labyrinth, a maze

Silver cobwebs spun on every door
I dare not enter, I dare not break
The delicate strings that hold together
Pieces of me…even as I flow.

## 6. Melting

A part of me is frozen
Icicles in my heart
Hardened clots of blood
Bits of pent up hurt, anger, rejection
Accumulated over the years
Locked up in an ice pack inside of me
In a deep dark space
A place I dread to visit
A place I call my hell

Yet those bits are as much me
As are the loving, happy bits
The soft, warm and fuzzy bits
Do I want to live in pieces or do I want to be whole?

It is a long road, there are no shortcuts here
I need to face my demons
Look them in the eye
Open up my wounds, wash them with tears
Then kiss them dry

I remember this
I felt like creeping into a deep black hole and dying
But I had to go on
So I locked up my pain into a box
And pushed it away
And there it slowly froze
And turned to ice

And there I forgot it
Until one day
A voice inside me
Whispered from the dark and dusty corners of my soul
It said to me:
"Your brokenness is beautiful
It's ok to cry
It's ok to feel the pain
It's ok to want to curl up like a caterpillar inside a cocoon
It's ok to want to vanish into thin air
It's ok to wish for unbound love
It's going to be ok"

And slowly as I feel the pain
Daggers stabbing through my flesh and blood
Arrows piercing my spirit
The tears start to flow
The knots of anguish clench and unclench
Until that moment of release when love
Slowly enters through the cracks of my broken self
And starts to fill that dark space

When the time is right
I will start to heal.

## 7. Seeking

I look up at the night sky with a deep longing
To see the stars, I search, I seek
I yearn for just a glimpse of shimmer in the blackness

Years go by, I keep looking
Until one day I realize
The sky is this external world
The star is my worth

How desperately I have tried to find it
Or even a sliver of it, outside
But now, I know better

I turn my gaze within
In a fleeting moment I see
The cosmos shining inside me
Constellations bursting forth in glory

I am mesmerized, I am humbled
I bow to Grace, I look up again
This time
The sky is studded with stars.

## 8. Breakthrough

Its scary down there
Deep in the abyss of nothingness
Where you feel you are nothing but the demons
That haunt you and drum the daylights out of you
You find yourself all alone
Fear grips your bones
You are afraid of being trapped in this dark hell-space forever
You fear that the chains that hold you hostage in the prison of your emptiness
Might never release their hold

You begin to wonder why you are alive
You begin to wait for death to come

We, the brave souls
Who have been thrown into
Or, with sacred intention, taken the plunge into
The horrific valleys of our darkness
We must learn to trust that this terror is a sign of our awakening
The burning desire within us
To grow, to shed the layers of our conditioning
Nudges us, pushes us, forces us
To the edge of the cliff of our comforts
Until we lose our footing
Start to fall
Feel the pain of daggers piercing the chest
Bleeding its primordial wound

In that moment
We look up to catch a glimpse of the sun, the sky
Make sure it's there
Nothing but the smoke of the ashes we are sitting in
Hovers above, the black lava oozing
From the volcano of our psychic being
Melting hot, peeling away the skin of our shallow
Existence to reveal the tender pink flesh of
A consciousness waiting to be awakened
A soul fire, waiting to be ignited.

## 9. Blue Horizon

That space where the Heavens meet the Earth
I find my Presence there
As much the trees, leaves and breeze
I'm also the stars and skies
There burns in me a fire wild
A silver lining also shines
My heart in rhythm with the ocean-waves
And other times it dances to
The music of Angels that fly
I dwell above, I live below
That blue horizon that you see
That's where you'll find my soul and me.

## 10. Becoming

The beginning of my Becoming
This journey to the heart
From yonder mind
Is long, the night of ignorance
Is dark, the moon has gone to
Sleep

Just barely half-alive I feel, for within me
There lies a world yet
Unexplored, a spirit
Unawakened, a universe
Uncreated
Waiting to be born

Protected by the mighty shield
Of faith, a lamp of light burns
Deep inside the crevice
Of my soul, gently illuminating
The jagged edges of my being

Beyond,
The tempests rage and roar
Waves as high as mountains
Tall, touch the sky, try to engulf
Destroy, extinguish, drown
The stars, the fire
But fail

A powerful field of energy
Unites the heavens and the earth
Surrounds me, wraps itself around me
Weaves me into the fabric
Of this cosmic space
Keeps aglow my sacred oil
Keeps alive my blessed flame

Light upon light!

Light beckons, fear
Holds me back,
Light beckons, I take a step
Forward, into the abyss
Who knows what wondrous joys
Await my Awakening
The beginning, of my Becoming.

## 11. Deep Dive

Let go
Throw yourself
Into the abyss of your soul
Trust life
Take the plunge

You will see the darkest dungeons
But you will also catch a glimpse of
The highest heavens beneath you
As you rise

The deepest pain
And the most profound joy
Will be yours.

## 12. Life-strokes

Blue and purple paint
Trickles down the white washed wall
Black oozes out and smears the once fresh colour
From the bottom right corner
It is a mess
Or is it?
The splash of myriad colours
The mix of feelingful strokes of brush
Caress the grainy surface
And tickle the gaps
There is no end to reach
It's a play of colours
A game of becoming
A life of being
A stroke of genius
Brown cookies burn
Until the sugar turns to caramel
My tongue is sweet
Because the honey finds its way
To the taste buds from the hive
It is a journey
Of unbecoming.

## 13. Carry On

Black night, dark dreams
Silver butterflies flit inside my mind
Sit on velvet roses
Sip sweet nectar
Shimmering cobwebs fill the spaces in between
Fireflies glow on the tips of my cells
Where dust accumulates
And still raindrops sparkle
Muddy waters need a place to flow
Toxic pathways need cleansing

There is a softness to the sand
That fills the gaps inside my bones
It is warm and dry
Beach-like
Ropes of silken thread tie up my thoughts
That rise and fall
And sway like branches of a tree
Smooth black pebbles that cover the river bed
Are flowing in my blood
Like armed forces ready to fight
Ready to win

I race across the white and stark landscape of this story
The bridge that travels to my core
Has wooden ridges built to carry my burdens
This journey is a risky one

The butterflies are busy shedding their cocoons
The fireflies are drowning in their sunken glory
A sudden shower of paint
Colours ruin and reign
Destruction is not the name of the game
Carry on, my dear, carry on.

## 14. Fragile

Hanging by a thread
Nowhere to go
Nothing to do
Except breathe deeply
And wait for time to heal

And as you wait
Let the pain feel itself inside you
Let it intensify
Let the universe invade your mind

See the galaxies and suns and stars
Our planet earth, all living beings
Ever changing, ever transient

In this grand scheme of things
You are but a speck
In this vast design

Step back and see yourself
See yourself rising
You suffer not in vain

See the pain doing its work
Propelling you into a state of being
Called Surrender

You're no longer hanging by a thread
You're floating now
In this lightness of being

You are reaching the heavens
You have nothing to do
Nowhere to go.

## 15. Life Goes On...

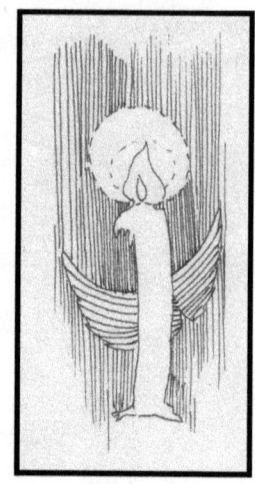

Flickering candle
Broken wings
A prayer right from the soul
Keep the light alive
Keep the wings from falling apart
I whisper with my deepest breath
The survival of the universe rests upon it
The candle burns on
The wings repair
Life goes on
In delight and in despair.

## 16. Paradox

The red of blood that drips from my deepest wounds
Gives colour to the scarlet rose
That blooms forth
From the soil of my being
And celebrates the awakening of spring

The subtle fragrance
Of a deeply meaningful life
That whiffs into my breath
Comes from the very scent
That emanates from the fragile surface
Of my broken spirit

The stark white blanket of snow
That covers up the soft green grass
Of my sunlit pasture of hope
Also brings pristine beauty
To the landscape of my dreams

The mighty waves of the vast blue sea
That leave the sailors mesmerized
By their sheer magnificence
Sometimes drown the most sturdy of ships

The heart that recedes
Like a snail into its shell
When it senses the pain of rejection
Opens up once again
At the slightest touch of love
Like a wild flower unfurling

It's all about potential
Enveloped in paradox
It's not what I have
But what I make of it

Joy carries within its folds
The shadow of sadness
The experience of sadness
Brings sensitivity to joy

We cannot truly know
The magic of light
Without having known
Darkness

We cannot catch a glimpse of hope
Without having been caught in the dungeon of despair

The one comes from the other
The other comes with the one
Both are needed
To live, to grow.

## 17. The River Story

These pebbles on the river bed
Smooth and rounded
Sharp and pointed
Black and white
Specked and grey
Tell a story of their own

A story of how it feels
To be stuck, then come lose
To be whirled around then be free to flow
A story of how grime and dust
Is cleaned and polished
Grain by grain
Day by day

A story of perseverance
In face of all forces
Strong as they may be
To be what you truly are
To find your real shape and form
To go where you rightly belong

They tell a story of their own.

## 18. Remembrance

Tangled threads of my being
Tug and pull
Ever-so-gently
The strings of my broken heart
And stir up the music
That softly awakens my soul
From the slumber
Of forgetfulness
Into the consciousness
Of remembrance
Whence follows a silence
Deeper
And more beautiful
Than any sound
Ever heard.

## 19. Elusive

You will not find me
In the transience of thoughts
That come and go
Nor in the fleeting glimpses of emotion
You will not see me in the movement of my limbs
Nor in the gentle sway of my body
You will not feel me in the sigh of my breath
Nor in the whisper of my words

You will find me
Deep inside within the self
In the permanence of my soul
Beyond the layers of body and mind
An eternal presence of faith
A being of love and joy

So come, step into this inner world
Where thoughts and movement
Tears and laughter
Dance and words
Fade away
And lose their grip on life
Step into this space that swells with gratitude
Join hands with me here

Never to part
Let our spirits unite
Let the silence speak out loud
And leave us in rapture

Leave all the conflict, the confusion
Drop it into the ocean
Let the salt of the sea of surrender cleanse you
And bring you closer to your truth

There is no looking back from here
Only rising to the stars
And merging with the light
No more distractions
No more wondering where to go
What to do, how to live, what to say

Crystal clear clarity abides
It takes us to the source of life
Makes us realize the glory of our existence
And humbles us all at once

The leaves fall from the trees
The boughs break
The trunk is axed

The roots decay
But the essence of the tree forever remains
Let's find that essence within ourselves
And stay there
In the safety of the promise of grace.

## 20. Topsy-Turvy

Drink up these bells they sway
Eat up the moon and stay
Roll up the hill and catch your breath
It's all a play

Don't you forget
Wake up tonight
And find your dream
Make peace and fight
Be calm, serene and scream

Life's topsy-turvy
We learn to cross the bridge
That stands below the salty sea
There is no rain but still it's wet

I wonder if the nightingale
Will spread its wings and fly

I want to say goodbye
To sorrows that keep haunting me
And yet I hesitate
My joyous laughter teases me
I dare not take the bait

Oh wild red rose
Blush not below the yellow sun
Let moonlight spill
And fill your petals soft and dark
Let's find a doorway
From this earth to heavens high

I sit alone
And thoughts of love and kindness
Float across the landscape of my mind
I let them be, like kites they sometimes
Tug and wrestle with the wind

A path that's narrow green and straight
With tulips growing on both sides
I touch the muddy stones
That lie beneath my feet

My hands are dirty like my mirror
I like them that way
Baked in clay
My hair is long and straight
Silky in its flow
And in its tresses lie locked the secrets of my soul.

## 21. Tie-in

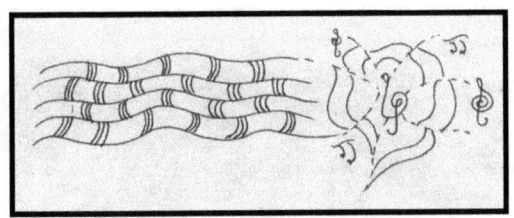

The free will of one man is the fate of another
We live within an intricate web of destiny
Tied up into each other like threads of a tapestry

While one surrenders
The other fights
One tries to break free
The other resists

The sooner we realize the better for us
That none can rise but with the rest
And none can fall alone

So let's be still yet awhile
Give time
The glorious colours will dance one day
To the music of unravelling mysteries

Light will come
Together we will shine.

## 22. Note from my soul to my heart

Tell me about the wounds you've buried
Deep within yourself
Show me the scars you haven't shown to anyone before
Let us together hold the sacred blood
That drips and softly stains the fabric of our being
Together feel the pain that's craving to be felt
Like a new-born yearning
To be held against her mother's breast

Let us together sit with the darkness of life
Like the forest sits still at night
Let us allow for the breaking of spirit
In a space of wholesome grace

Let us allow for crying
Let us allow for bleeding
Let us allow for healing

This storm within that's lying dormant
Let it rage and settle into the calmness of our hold

I'm here to hold your pain with you
I'm here to show up for life with you
I'm here to open heart, to feel, to flow
Hold hands and walk bare feet
Upon this sacred ground.

*Love*

## 23. Ever-lasting

Love is not a delicate twig
That will break with the rush of wind
Or a downpour of heavy rain

Love is strong roots, intertwined
Finding their way together
Towards the source of life

It is the solid bark that will not bend
Nor even shake
In the storm

Like rose-petals gentle and soft
But unlike them, love is not fragile
It is hardy and everlasting

Like the mountains
It is here to stay.

## 24. Give it Time

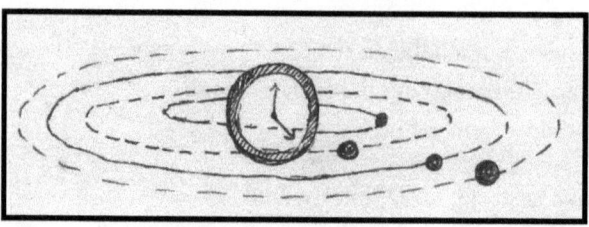

In the cosmic framework of time
There is no rush for anything to get done
Things happen when the moment is right
The universe will not run out of time

Let life take its course
If it is meant to be in this world
It will be

At the end of it all
When both of us transcend
The limitations of body and mind
Our spirits will unite

For after all
Your soul and mine
Is made of the same stuff

This is the consolation I offer myself
When I miss the love we shared.

## 25. Moments Live On

There is something between us still
Even if it's just the residue of past love

A long forgotten sweet fragrance
Of special moments shared
Momentarily dispels the ever lingering
Bitter taste of hurtful exchanges

I remember our handholding
From a tight clasp to a loose grip
To a slight touch of fingertips
To complete release

You are still you
I am still me
Times changed
And with it
We

Distracted by other pursuits
We drifted apart
And let each other fade away
From the map of our mind

We let our memories
Be re-written

Still, somewhere, some remnants
Of our long lost love
Remain

And when I happen to chance upon them
On a cold winter's night
For a fleeting moment, I feel warm
Even though the fire in the hearth
Has long burnt out.

## 26. Togetherness

The novelty, nor the fire
Of new love
Can compare to the seasoned flavour
Of love grown old

Nor the fiery glow of youth
To the matt richness of ripe age

Two people, old lovers
Who know the creases on each other's skin
The crevices of each other's soul

How each one looks in the morning
With the first opening of eyes
How each one speaks
When ashamed or filled with pride

How long they take
To sip their tea
The speck on their shoulder
That mark on their back

Oh the comfort of familiarity
The ease of informality
The passing of time in togetherness
Is like the perfect comfort of worn-out jeans

I await the coming of that moment
When I will swell with joy and say
I've been with you for five and twenty years.

## 27. Story of heartbreak

The heart dreams....
Perhaps it is the nature of the heart to dream

But many a times
Along with the dream, it breaks
Is that also part of its nature, I wonder

We love and we lose
And maybe we love again
But not as much as the stars that shine in a cloudless sky
On a quiet moonless night
That once-in-a-life-time kind of love
The one that gives life
To life

The heart is soft, the pain is hard
There is joy in love, sorrow in heartbreak
Joy and sorrow, like the seasons
Come and go
But love, it stays, it grows
It doesn't change, it doesn't go

Love becomes you, Love becomes me
You become me, We become one
How do I leave myself and go
Where do I find a different me
The one that does not remember
How it felt to be the kiss that never left your lips

I am here
Love is my home
There is no other place for me to be

I reach out my hand for you to hold it
I see your hands are tied
Hope and I cling on to each other
I look at you
I ask, "Will you be mine?"
I wait for an answer
Not a promise, just a word

You look at me silently, helplessly
Until a teardrop slowly slides down my cheek
The melting of my dream

So much is left unsaid
So much yet to be done
So many ways to love you still

The road is long, I travel alone
The journey is mine, I have to go on
A loneliness envelops me
I lay down, I go to sleep, I dream

When I wake up
The taste of salt upon my lips
A wetness on my face

I look above
The moon is floating in the sky
The moonlight shines upon a pebble close
I take it in my hand
It is smooth

It is cold, like the distance between us

Slowly one by one, illusions break
They fall apart like crumbled pieces of pie
I stand and stare
What is real, what is not

The world plays tricks
We get caught up in its games
I'm tired;  I have no interest in winning
No fear of losing
I just want to breathe
Just want to love

People can have their trophies
I would rather have my peace
The peace that lies waiting for me somewhere
Beyond the broken dream
Beyond my broken heart

I carry on, I walk along
The love inside me as alive as ever it has been
I walk along barefeet upon the sandy ground
My footprints tell a story of their own
I walk along
And as I cry, I also pray
Keep my beloved in Your care.....

## 28. Beyond a Crescent

The moon is full tonight, almost
As full as our love
But not quite

From a sliver
To a crescent
To a half
To a whole

Our love grew and still it grows
A bit more everyday
Unlike the moon
It will not wane

The laws of love
How beautifully they break, nay
Transcend
The laws of nature.

## 29. Wholeness

We fit into each other
Like two pieces of a puzzle, yet
Unlike a puzzle
We will never be done with and complete
We will continue to discover and see
New parts of you and me
For in between the both of us
There is still space to grow
To find missing pieces of ourselves
In our seeking to become whole.

## 30. It's All There Is

It comes to me in flashes of lightning
This image of eternal love
Where time and space, they slip away
And all that's left is love

A yearning deep within the soul
Beyond the realm of thought and mind
The will to love, the want to be loved
Strong, powerful and intense
Both will and want, they fade away
And what remains is love

So beautiful and rare it is
A dewdrop shining in the sun
The drop, it slips into the earth
The sun, it sets into the west
What's left is only love.

## 31. To My Child

He gave you unto me, my child
Entrusted to my care, you came
Out of my womb, into my arms
To hold and love with all my heart
To share with you the gift of faith
To see the light within you shine
Then gently, when the time is right
To let you go and find your way

Until the time we meet again
Beyond the bounds of time and space.

## 32. Broken Wings

The dancing flowers of yesterday
Now buried deep beneath the snow
The music of the summer wind
Drowned in winter's piercing echo of doom

Broken wings of butterflies
Lie still upon the frosted window pane

The moment we opened our hearts to love
Has passed, light has gone
Darkness descends
Upon a cold white stark reality

I close my eyes
I whisper a prayer
I breathe

A flickering candle burns
Life goes on.

## 33. Sakina's Portrait
(Sakina is my beloved daughter)

Dripping innocence, liquid eyes
Speak to me in a hundred
Different languages, say
To me a thousand different words
Untold stories of 'Once upon a time'…

Arched eyebrows, gently raised
Wonder: what is this feeling?
Evocative yet evanescent
Fleeting yet full

Nose like a bridge, dainty
But daring
Playful like a parrot
On a swing

Strawberry pink
Blooming cheeks, ripe
In their season of youth
Springtime has come
Be merry and dance my girl

She looks at me
I look at her, this memory

Will not fade
Soft lips tilt slightly
At the corners, a moment's
Melancholy smile
Captured forever
Here
In this portrait of my precious girl.

## 34. Wish Fulfilled

The night is dark
The sky is purple-black
There is no moon, there are no stars
A silky stillness fills the air
I breathe

Your name escapes my lips

Softly
The silence is broken
Slowly
A quiet corner of my soul
Lights up
A fragrance ever-so-sweet
Finds its way
Into my heart

My spirit starts to fly
I soar up high into the sky
I leave behind a silver lining in the clouds
I reach the moon and lo behold
I find you there

From far beyond
To seek me you have come
For when your name
Escaped my lips
Unknowing to your conscious mind
Your soul set out to search for me
It found me in the realm of stars
Where I had come to look for you

The both of us
We melt into the stardust now

And as we meet
The heavens weep to see us two
Who left the earth and made our way
Beyond the darkness of the night
Beyond the black and purple skies
To find a way to be together
In a world beyond the one
We live in now

Now here we are amongst the stars
Let's dance a while
Before its time to separate
Before its time to go back down
Let's for some moments make the most
Of being in this starry bliss
Let's for some moments just pretend
The moon is our nesting home.

## 35. Loved and Lost....

"Tis better to have loved and lost than not
Have loved at all," they say
And humbly I do agree, you see
Love's being caught
Inside a web from which it's hard to flee
A niche so sacred, deep and full of soul
A place that's filled with rapture and with pain
You're broken, yet you've never felt more whole
You feel like dancing all night long in rain
To love is to be willing to lay out
Your heart upon the table, fresh and bare
Just like in faith there is no place for doubt
In love there's only hope, there's no despair
"Tis better to have loved and lost," I say
"Than not have loved," it is the only way.

## 36. Could It Be

Could it be
That the oceans wonder
At the deep secrets in your eyes

Could it be
That the peaks of mountains long to meet the valleys below
The way my spirit longs to embrace yours

Could it be
That spring longs to merge into autumn
Bright colour flowers into bright colour leaves
The way I wish to melt into your hold

Could it be
That the dark night of my story seeks comfort
In the light of your soul

Could it be
That somewhere in a parallel universe
You and I are dancing
To the tune of our favourite song

Could it be
That between beginnings and endings
There are spaces called Eternity
Waiting to be discovered by you and me.

*Nature*

## 37. Lie. Breathe. Bliss.

Canopy of trees and clouds above
Bed of soil and dried leaves below
Crisp air filled with butter sunlight
Sandwiched in between
Somewhere in this layered heaven
I lie
I breathe
I bliss.

## 38. Walk in Matheran

Rich and rusty
Winding dirt-path
Dried leaves, round pebbles

Gnarled and knotted roots
Emerging proudly
Like warriors
From beneath the rugged trail

Thick crusted tree trunks
Looming large
Like giants' limbs

Serpent-like branches
Reach up high
Stretch, like a newly awakened maiden
To touch the sky
A sweep of wholesome emptiness
Not a whiff of cloud

Butter-yellow rays of life
Fall gently
Upon the leaves
Dancing shadows
Flitting back and forth
Across the path, the trees

Silent silhouettes

Move through the forest
Walk by the woods
Now fast, now slow
Tripping over a stone there
Hopping over a boulder here
Supple forms trek on

Stop and listen
Sound of crickets
Soft rustle of leaves
Shallow breath

Stop and look
Stop and wonder
Steal a glance
Deep valley below
Miss a heartbeat or two
Then carry on....

## 39. Symphony

Twitter of birds
In the crisp cool morn
Rustle of leaves
In the warm afternoon breeze
Whisper of your breath
Under the translucent moon
All remind me
That even as the music of the heavens
Echoes in the sky
The earth is filled
With a music of its own.

# 40. Play

Lying down
Upon the forest floor
A bed of dried twigs and soil
A blanket of woody moistness covers me

From in between the broken gaps
Of twisted branches overhead
I see the sky in pieces and bits
Geometric shapes in shades of blue

Soft rustle of leaves
Competes
With sound of crickets
To tease away the sultry silence

Immersed into my element
I let the sunlight
Play on me
The shadows
Sway on me

Immersed into this earthiness
I become the forest
The forest becomes me.

# 41. Rider

The sound of wind
The beat of hooves
The rhythmic blowing of my horse

Flying above the grass
She gallops across the field
In beauty and powerful grace

The land before her bows in awe
The sky above begins to crave
The touch of her shoe
The brush of her mane

I feel humbled
To be carried by this magnificent beast
So perfect in its form

I feel proud to be called a rider.

## 42. Home

I find myself
Walking barefoot
On a narrow dirt road
*I find myself at home*

High up
On the banyan tree
Sitting a bit precariously
*I find myself at home*

*Feeling the pulse of the earth beneath*
*As I lie on a bed*
*Of dried up twigs and leaves*
*I feel I am home*

Ice-cold river
Water comes alive and flows
I take a dip
*I feel I am home*

Hay all around
Smell of horse
Sound of hooves
I groom my mare
*I feel at home*

Lovingly, you hold me
In your arms
Nowhere to go
This is my dwelling
*You are my home.*

## 43. Peeling

Times fall apart
Like days-old bread
Crumbling into little bits

Furry flakes of memories
Float by
Some stick like glue
Some fly away
Only to come crashing back
Like waves on jagged rocks

Grey and purple shadows
Dart across the landscape of my dreams
Bruises are also the colour red
But mine do not bleed
For I have signed a truce
With my wounded soul

Those cobwebs
They no longer fill up
Empty spaces of my mind
The stuff which I carry inside my heart
Is light
Like beaten-whites of eggs

I sing-along with the stream
As it gurgles past
I sing of times gone by
And those to come

I praise the sky
From whence the raindrops fall
And wash away the remnants
Of the layers that cover me
Like moss
From the bark of a tree.

## 44. Tree Talk

I whisper my secrets to the tree
It never gives them away

I say to it
All that I wish
I share with it
My hopes and dreams

Silently
It listens to me
Quietly
It lets me be

I whisper my secrets to the tree
It never gives them away

It keeps them safe inside its roots
Below the earth
Where none can see
Beneath the soil
Where none can hear

I whisper my secrets to the tree
It never gives them away

And when the tree
Begins to flower
The flowers
Begin to bloom

The fragrance sweet
Of secrets shared
Comes home to me upon the breeze
And fills my breath

I whisper my secrets to the tree
It offers them back to me.

## 45. Virgin Eyes

Every time I look
I see it as if for the very first time

Green, yellow, rust, brown
Sprinkled with golden rays of sun

Fresh and dried leaves
Twisted branches
Hanging roots
Lush forest

I've walked this path
A hundred times
Yet, the sense of wonderment
Strikes anew each time
With each step
I'm left in awe
Of this paradise
Offered by Mother Earth

This miracle of nature
Consecrated
By the sun, rain and wind

It lifts up my spirit
Lights up my eyes
Instils in me
A sense of pride

And hope
One that only sublime beauty
Can evoke

A reassurance
That everything will be alright.

# 46. Coming Back to Myself

Waves of this magnificent ocean
Let me dissolve my spirit into yours

Let me flow
With the currents
Go where they go
Take me off to far away lands

Let me melt into the foam
That washes up the shores
Of tropical lands
On the edges of the earth

Let me rejuvenate
And shimmer on the surface
With the reflection of
Burning rays

Then after this process
Of dying and rebirth
Give my essence back to me

I will be standing here
Waiting by the sea.

## 47. Dream-catcher

The night is cool, dark and musical
I can hear the sound of rain
The water-droplets dancing as they touch the ground
I close my eyes and quietly listen....
What messages do the raindrops
Bring from high up in the skies?
What secrets of the heavens
Do they whisper to the seas?
Then slowly as I drift to sleep
I hear their stories in my ear
Of stars and moons

And how each one says to the clouds
When you go down upon the earth
Be sure to take me with you once
I too would like to kiss the earth
And lean and glide upon the trees

Then when the sun comes up next day
I'll catch a ride on one of its rays
And find my way back to the sky....

And as I dream, I see myself
All wet and dancing in the rain

Then slowly I begin to rise
And float up high into the sky
And there I greet the clouds before
I go up higher to the stars
They twinkle right into my face
Their stardust sprinkling over me
Until I'm glowing in the dark

Slowly the sunlight scatters now
I better get back to my bed
Before they notice I'm gone

Like raindrops falling from the sky
I fall upon a rainbow slide
Then land upon a treetop high
Where larks and cuckoos sing for me
A song of joy and fun and glee
And when it's done
I climb right down into my cosy bed
And float into the sweetest sleep.

## 48. Slice of Orange Moon

Oh breath-taking beauty of nature
Relieve the burden of sorrows
That weighs down upon my heart

As I look at the raindrops falling
Like a string of pearls from yonder heaven
See the ocean in its glory
Magnificent rolling waves
Stare in awe at the star-studded night sky
The slice-of-orange moon

Within my heart a burden lifts
A darkness breaks into dawn
The magic of nature brings joy
To the most woeful heart

A treat for weary eyes
A balm for weary souls

A sip of cool water for the thirsty spirit
A gentle caress
For the heart that's wounded

A constant reminder
That there is hope
There is beauty
Inside ourselves and out
For what we see outside
Is but a reflection of our inner being
Which in its most natural form
Is a manifestation of the Divine.

## 49. Soaked

Warm waves of sunlight
Wash over my face

I soak it up
I let it seep
Through my skin
Into my soul

From whence
The light within me shines
Radiates outside
Embraces the spark that brings it to life

What a delight
This fusion of energy
What a dazzle
This union of soul and star.

## 50. Ripe Corn and Snow

One half of me sees sunshine
Pretty flowers dancing in the breeze
The rustling sound of swaying leaves
And beautiful evergreen trees

The other half, it sees a storm
Thunder and lightning too
Sky is roaring, rain is pouring
Dark black night, no trace of light

But deep inside the wakeful presence that I am
All parts are held together
All things are seen at once
Contradictions fade away
Darkness merges into light

Summer and storm
Walk hand in hand
Upon a field of sun, ripe corn and snow.

## 51. Immersed

The waves-like sound
Of blowing wind
Break the soft silence
Of the forest

Hazel eyes
Share their color
With the leaves

Heart beats
With the symphony
Of the trees

Warm rays of sunlight
Shadows dancing
In the cool breeze

Musty smell of earth
Faint buzz of insects
Crickets half-asleep

I lay still
Upon a bed of soil
Pebbles and dried twigs
I set my spirit free.

## 52. Journey

I swim in the ocean
I swish in the sea
The waves they cherish my touch
I feel the coolness
On the warmth of my skin
Supple body
Fully immersed
Soaking up the salt
Soaking up the roar
No shore in sight
This is where I belong

From here I fly
High into the sky
Past the clouds
To the moon and the stars
The silence wraps me into its arms
I float like a leaf in the wind
I feel the peace, I feel the calm
I stretch my arms out wide
This is my moment.

## 53. An Affair to Remember

Once upon a time…
I had an affair
And in my heart it still goes on
He was handsome, tall and dark
Muscle defined his skin
His eyes held depths of oceans green
His mouth was soft as a rose

I remember our walk through the field that day
Me and him alone
Not a word was spoken
The silence was broken
Only by the sound of his breath

He carried me with powerful grace
I felt secure, I felt so safe
I felt like a cloud floating in the sky
I felt like a ship on calm blue seas
I felt joy and peace in my soul

Between us a bond, as strong as faith
Complete understanding too
I knew he loved me, I loved him more
His noble self so full of trust
So full of honor and gentleness
No more did I ask for

Undaunted by the mountains high
He climbed right on with steadfast gait
The world with all its forests and lakes
For him a wandering place.
His stride was so majestic and grand
His strength was overflowing grace
So humbled by his form I was
I bowed in his embrace

I still can feel his body bare
To yearn for more I do not dare
His velvet touch, his flowing hair
I held on to it strong and tight
I held to him with all my might
We lived in a world of our own

'Twas him and me
Out on the fields
The wind was playing music sweet
As if my fingers and my toes
Wore bells and ribbons tied in bows

The morning turned to afternoon
The afternoon to night
But for us time stood still as though
Each moment came but didn't go
Each moment came with feelings fresh
Each feeling filled with passions raw
We kept afloat and yet we drowned
In oceans of desire

My longing for him knew no end
I'm still enveloped in his scent

My horse, so beautiful so brown
My king he is, my love his crown
I love him so forever… I
Remember his and my affair
It still goes on and on and on…
In my true heart, forever more.

# Life

## 54. What's the Question

Crystal chandeliers
Reflecting colours that etch my memory
With strokes of acruylic stardust
I fill my cup with the left over pieces of time
Brimful in its poignancy
The waiting will end soon

The sky is silver green tonight
The moon is red
Fire blazes and burns the papers
That hold the story of my life
The ashes flat up in the air
Landing upon my nose and forehead

Sticky senses follow me
The barking kettle will not let me sip
The tea I crave for in my dreams
The sleepy sunlight mellow and thick with brightness
Dipping down into the ocean's
Orange and pink salty waters
Beauty unsurpassed

Seaweeds entangled into a puff of soupy crust
Seagulls circle, draining patterns of infamiliar numbers
and words

Let's get to the bottom of it all
Enough fluff and candy
What's the deal
The question echoes
From one edge of the universe to the other
"Will you be coming home tonight?"

## 55. Hawk

Stop seeking and searching
Like a hawk ready to prey
Fold your wings
Perch on a branch
Close your eyes
Let it come to you
The feeling of wholesome nothingness
And wilful ease
Let your stillness melt
And glide into the cloud like a silver lining
Now open your eyes
Now spread your wings
Now soar the skies.

## 56. Free-fall

Falling off a cliff
And I'm loving it
The valley below me opens its arms
I wait for my body
To touch the ground and explode
But in that moment of surrender
Something happens
Call it grace
Call it miracle
I begin to float like a feather
The laws of gravity bow down
To the laws of faith
I feel a lightness of being
That makes me wonder:
Am I still alive
Or is it the rapture of death that envelops me
My eyes can see the green earth
The blue sky
The red soil and purple stone of the mountainside
The illusion of bleakness dissolves
Into a canvas of carbon colors
Waiting to be discovered
I see it now
I fly I feel I find a hand
Holding my own
I bend I kneel I bow
All this - mind you - in mid air

I sleep I dream I wake up
Time stretches
Like an elastic band
And I stretch with it
Long complicated questions
Have but simple one word answers
"Open my heart
Bring me home."

## 57. Piercings

Sticks pierce my skin
And leave scars
Sometimes blood-red
Roses caress me
They heal
Transform the bruises
Into magnificent artwork

I wonder at this mystery
Now a broken object, now a masterpiece

Sticks and stones
Thorns and petals
Water and sawdust
One bringing me to another
All giving and receiving
According to the laws of nature

Peppermint leaves
Sprigs of Japanese cherry blossom
Clover with its distinct smell
All that you can think of

My life has its own twists and turns
I live in this shadowy dance theatre
Where things keep changing
Happening slowly at first
Then fast

I watch my character
Move through the scenes
With the sticks
With the puppets
With the people

Dancing, crying
Wailing, singing
All of it
Buckets of it
Lists of dreams spilling over
Onto a canvas
That cannot hold anymore colour
It is so full
And heavy
Almost cracking from the weight
Of the paint

The black curtain falls
Now it's time to rest
Just fall back and close eyes
Feel the soft petals
As they brush against the softness
Of your breath
My breath
What difference does it make
Whether it's you or me

The sticks that pierce me leave their mark on you
The warmth that envelops you
Sets me on fire
For these things know no boundaries
They just flow freely

Like energy
Sunlight to water
Water to air
Air to fire
And earth.

Mingling in their web of
Collectivity
Brazen desire
Tugging them in all directions
Until they let go of all resistance
And dissolve
Into the fullness of the cosmos
Into the nothingness of space.

## 58. Mindful Emptiness

Scattered thoughts
Cluttered mind
I need to sit in a dark room
In silence
And sort out my life

Gathered thoughts
Clear mind
I want to sit in a quiet place
In silence
And reflect upon my life

Empty thoughts
Empty mind
I wish to sit on sunlit grass
In silence
And celebrate my life.

## 59. Rainbow in the puddle

Blue green violet
Colour my mind with strokes of genius
It's a dragon that comes alive within
The smoky fire breathes in me
My destiny
Charcoal petals soft and black
Smear my face
The tears have long dried
Beautiful eyes dissolve into their own mystery
Where is the door
Or is there one
Maybe just a window
With frilled curtains
Looking upon the meadows
Yellow sunlight pouring in
Into my coffee cup
I sip
I smile to think of all the joys
That overflow
And spill into my life

Sounds of laughter echo deep inside
The well of wishful memories
Buckets and buckets of dreams
The world spins
And with it my mind.

## 60. My Father

He walks no more
Upon this earth
The ground
It weeps

He breathes no more
The air
Is thick with grief

He stands no more
Beneath the tree
The leaves and boughs
Feel blue

Will he never again
My forehead kiss?
Or gently caress
With his palm, my cheek?

Now, in that place
Where he touched my face
My tears softly flow.

## 61. Long time ago

Sharing one plate
We ate
Sharing one glass
We drank
From the same book
We read
With the same toy
We played.

We ran
On the same grass
Walked
On the same path
Danced
In the same rain
Singing
The same song

We lived together
Side by side
Now who's that stranger walking past?

## 62. Useful Reminders

In my teens, I used to remind myself
To put cream on my face and kohl in my eyes
To wear the pretty bangles and my silver ring
To watch the movie starring my favourite actor
Also study, please others and do what is right

In my twenties I reminded myself
To remember that I am blessed
To carry money when I left the house
To eat a banana, keep hydrated
To pack the orange scarf that I like so much
And of course, make sure I'm liked

As I came into my thirties
I reminded myself to be patient and calm
And above all, kind
I told myself that the struggles in life
Are meant to help me grow
I reminded myself that I need to be strong
To work on myself and become better
And not be concerned about what
others think of me

I reminded myself to be me
But I didn't know who I was

And now, as I go through my forties
My reminders have once again changed

I remind myself to let go, to trust life
I invite myself to witness
And accept with loving compassion
All the different parts of me
Light and darkness
Clarity and chaos
Anger and peace
I remind myself to reflect and ask
"Where were you before you came into human form?
You've been taken care of long before you were born."

The most profound logic
That supports the soul's safety and worth
Lies in the laws of existence, I say to myself
For now these are good reminders.

## 63. Invisible Tattoos

Invisible tattoos cover my skin
Stories of the life I've lived so far

Somewhere a horse
Runs wild and free
Somewhere a caged bird
Wants to sing

Somewhere a monster
Wants to roar
Somewhere a calm
And quiet shore

Somewhere a circus full of kids
Somewhere an empty yard
Somewhere there's blood
Where the cactus pricks
Somewhere a soft red rose

Somewhere there is a pile of dust
Somewhere a broken library
Somewhere the moon is shining bright
Somewhere the dark night lurks

Somewhere high walls imprison me
Somewhere there is an open field
Somewhere the ghosts of a haunted past
Somewhere the hopes of a sunlit dream

Somewhere the sun is dipping down
Somewhere the rise of a dazzling dawn

The pictures pale
The outlines fade

My teardrops fall and smear the ink
And leave it all a-blur.

## 64. Paint

Blue ribbons strewn across
The landscape of my dreams
Yellow lights dance upon
The canvas of my life

Crimson petals sprinkled on
Unspoken words of poetry
Orange leaves, they fall from trees
And land upon the scattered dust
Of my crumbled soul

Crimson, orange, yellow and blue
All colours fade into the dusk
I take a breath
Inhale the darkness of the night

And with the air that I exhale
A thousand colours spill into
And lighten up the autumn sky
There is no need for the harvest moon tonight.

## 65. Wholesome Existence

I live in many places
All at once

In the warmth of a smile that I share
With a happy stranger walking by
I momentarily come alive
Then slowly fade away

In a half-full cup of sugarless tea
A torn but well-worn riding shirt
A crumbling piece of left-over pie
The essence of me
Lingers

In the blooming of a rose
My eyes chance to feast upon
In the dew of the grass
My bare feet walk on
I am

I live in the roar of the ocean
The silence of the caves
In the wind that plays with my hair
The breeze that carries my scent

Raindrops
That trickle down my head, face and arms
Before they touch the ground

I live in the tree I hug
In the warmth of the sunrays
That gently wash my face

And all of them
They live in me.

## 66. Joy of Work

Without the toil of hard labour
Without the ploughing and tilling
The sowing and sweating
The watering and weeding
The pruning and plucking

Without the faith
That sun will shine
And rain will fall

The reaping of fruits in harvest
Would not bring such cheer
To the face of the farmer.

## 67. Insatiable

If we could
We would cut up the sky into pieces
And salvage the stars from the heavens
Divide the rays of the sun
And moon

This light is mine
That light is yours

Just like we've cut this earth
And sliced it up
This land is mine
That island yours
That territory belongs to them

We fight to possess our planet
As though it is us
Who have created it

Is there a limit to the selfishness
Of man
Is there an end to his pride?

## 68. Abuse

You left
Your fingerprints
Over my body
Stamped your footprints
On my soul

You
Touched my body
Not with love
Crushed my spirit
Wrecked my soul.

## 69. A Woman

Soft yet strong
Calm yet vibrant
Simple but stunning

A nurturer of life
A giver of love
A bearer of hardships
A keeper of faith

A tigress in her ferocity
A lamb in her gentleness
Graceful as a doe.

## 70. It Simply Is

Beautiful as ever
The rose blooms
Not a whiff of arrogance
Touches its fragrance

And when it withers
It does not sulk nor moan
It simply dries, crumbles
And falls to the earth
Becomes the soil

Until slowly
Someday, who knows
It might find its way
Back to the roots
Up the stem
To the blooming bud

No strife, no conflict
No craving, nor complaint
Only sheer content, wonderful,
Divinely sublime existence.

## 71. Fantasy

I'm floating in the sky above
The sound of music in the air
I twirl around the clouds with joy
The silver lining twists and turns
And joins me in my dance

The rainbow colours laugh with me
The birds they greet me as they fly
The sunshine washes over me
It bathes me in its warmth
A feeling of elated blissness
Soaks itself into my skin

As I look down upon the earth
A field of butter daffodils
All swaying softly in the breeze
The snow clad mountain peaks below
Like ice-cream on a lopside cone

And suddenly as I float on
I chance upon a pink and fuzzy unicorn
It beckons me to climb on it and takes off on a flight
We glide across the creamy sky
I hang on to its silky mane

And lo behold, out of the blue
Lil drops of glitter start to rain
They fall upon me, make me shine

As I dismount upon a puff
And there before me dark and smooth
A chocolate fountain rises up
I dip a finger into it
And put it in my mouth

And when night falls, the stars alight
And sprinkle me with stardust bright
The moon comes up and whispers in
My ear the secrets of its dream
A bed of flower petals now
I see before me as I slide
Right into it and curl up tight
And close my eyes and fall asleep
Then in my sleep I smile.

## 72. Flow

Life, it happens
It happens while we're busy
Cleaning the closet
Or standing on the roadside waiting for a cab
It happens while we worry about paying the bills
Or while we're arguing
With the mailman
Or buying groceries at a crowded supermarket

It happens while the world around us falls apart
And we fight desperately
To keep ouselves from going insane

It keeps happening
While we're sleeping
Or crying or laughing or sneezing
Or drinking a cup of dark hot chocolate
On a cool autumn night
Or walking barefeet upon a sandy beach on a sunny day
Moments when we wish for time to pause
But it doesn't, not for a minute

Life keeps happening
Sometimes fast, sometimes slow, sometimes faster
It happens
Beautifully
When we live and love with an open heart
Amazingly

When we laugh with friends
Wonderfully
When we rejoice and sing
Soulfully
When we surrender and pray

Alas,
It happens woefully
When we get caught up in our worries
And forget to smile
Regretfully
While we're busy with work
And our kids give up on seeking our attention
Before we know it they've grown up and gone.

Days darken into nights
Nights brighten into days
Life happens and keeps happening

But when you or I or any passer-by
Stops for a moment
To hold a hand
To give a ear
Or share a smile
That's when life basks in the glory
Of overflowing grace
And in those precious moments
Life becomes priceless, time becomes eternal.

# 73. In His Shoes

Just for a moment
Close your eyes
Bear with me through this exercise

Picture a child
Sitting on the footpath
Dressed in rags
Unkempt hair
Dirty hands
Weeping silently for want of food
Not a morsel to eat
The life in him
Slowly seeping out

Now open your eyes
Come back to here
Can you go on living
The way you did before?

## 74. Spoonful of Indifference

It all begins in the mind
Wars and genocides
Terrorist attacks and bombings
All born in the mind with the germ of an idea
Passions, ideologies, instincts
Manifesting into action
Violent reactions
Affecting one or ten or hundred or thousands of people
For good or bad, better or worst
People live, people die
Some stay in limbo, neither alive nor dead
But numbers don't matter
No one keeps count
Everyone's too busy with their own lives
Sipping their cup of coffee or tea -
Just a spoonful of sugar but no cream please.

## 75. Cry No More

I can feel your silent tears
Burn like acid through the fabric of my heart
And scorch my soul

I can sense your pain, your anguish
Like shards of glass
Piercing my flesh

I can see your scarred face
The trauma in your eyes
Haunting me at every turn of the road

I know you are broken
I know you have lost all hope
You feel you are being tossed around
Like a dinghy on rough seas

I wish I could be your anchor
I wish I could hold your hand
And tell you only these two lines:
"You are loved, my dear
More than you will ever know."

## 76. Wonder

Aah! That moment
When you chance upon
A child dressed in rags
With a beaming smile on his face
And wonder at the beauty of contentment

Aah! That moment
When you chance upon
A lotus blooming in muddy water
And wonder at the miracle of transformation

Aah! That moment
When you chance upon
A cherished, long-forgotten memory
And wonder at the passing of time

Aah! That moment
When you chance upon
A smile with crinkles at the corners of the eyes
And wonder at the charm of wisdom

Aah! That moment
When you chance upon
A strong desire in your heart
A will to move mountains

Courage to win hearts
And wonder at the burning fire of passion

Aah! That moment
When you chance upon
A stillness within
A deep sense of peace and calm
And wonder at the joy of surrender.

## 77. Caving In

I can feel myself slipping
From solid to shaky ground
I can feel doubts and uncertainties
Creep in to push out faith and hope
I can feel the mind working
Emotions churning
The soul receding from the edges
Of my being into its shell
There's too much noise here
Too much resistance
From life to flow

I find myself
Slipping down the slope
Away from the space of soul
Into the abyss of confusion
Soul in its shell
Chaos outside
Storms brewing, passions wrecking
Wailing and piercing shrieks
No room for soul to flow

Inside its own space, it then abides
In alignment with the laws of the universe
It remains steadfast
In face of earthquakes and storms
It knows there is no gain
In becoming part of this game

This drama, this delusion
Where the essence of life is lost
Caught up in rights and wrongs
Caught up in worries and woes
Going round and round in circles
In the illusion of getting somewhere
When in reality there is nowhere to go

Perhaps silence is the only way
For the soul to spread out
Into the fibre of my being
To permeate the crevices and corners
Of the heart and mind
So that emotion does not conjure passion
And thought does not create confusion
The heart will have faith
The mind will have clarity
The physical being itself
Will feel light as a spirit

All this when the soul comes out
Of its shell and suffuses itself into all of me.

## 78. Shine I will

(Inspired by Maya Angelou's Still I Rise)

With ashes and soot, you may tarnish my name
Your words and looks, my honour defame
Yet, like the stars on a moonless night
Shine, I will

You may use your worldly power and design
To deal me blows that bruise my heart and mind
Yet like the moon in a cloudless sky
Shine, I will

Your apparent victory may crush
The gentle fabric of my soul
Your shouts of rage may bury
The whisper of my sobs, the silence of my pain
Yet, like the candle burning in the dark
Shine, I will

The shadows you cast upon me cannot dull my spirit
The echoes of our past do not haunt me now
Like the embers that glow when the fire has died
Shine I will

I will shine like the sun, the moon, the stars
I will shine like a candle burning bright
I will shine with the glow of courage and faith
I will shine with the radiance of truth and hope
Shine I will

Forever I will shine, my dreams will shine
My fortunes will shine, and when unto the dust
I shall return, I will still be alive
For the love I leave, the memories I bequeath
Will eternally sparkle and shine.

## 79. From Rage To Redemption

Behold! I come in all my brokenness
As you can see - my light is all but gone
The crown upon my head that glory held
Is now reduced to ashes, and the silk
That wove itself around my waist replaced
By coarse black ropes that choke my gut inside
As fate draws me e'er closer to its jaw.

There was a time when stars were at my feet
And now the blood that oozes out in spurts
The agony that splits and cracks my bones
Light up a fire dark and red as coals
I hear the chanting all around me rise
"We want her dead, we want her dead," they cry.

The anger in me aches to shut their mouths
And stuff them up with sawdust, as I break
The chains that clamp my neck, my hands, my legs;
A thunderbolt within me starts to grow
It threatens to destroy the evil lies
That float like poison in the air, I long
To draw the sword of truth and pierce my chest
For them to see the golden heart that beats
Inside my bosom, nesting deep at peace
I cannot breathe, yet life hangs on to me
My soul then whispers silently, "Oh Lord!
Forgive them for they know not what they do."

## 80. Silver in Grey

In search of breath, I gasp and gulp for air
My eyes, my nose, my mouth are parched and dry
My heart feels heavy, soul is laid out bare
I cannot scream or shout, I dare not cry
I fall down on my knees, I start to pray
Amidst the crumbled pieces of my life
I search for silver linings in the grey
I look for joyous times within the strife
This darkness that envelops me is mine
Someday the sun will rise in me and shine.

## 81. Innocence Lost

Innocent hearts
Innocent faces
Innocent eyes
Filled with hurt, anger, confusion
Look at me helplessly

Struggling with a barrage of mixed thoughts
Churning emotions
Caught up in the conundrum
Of this cruel world

Little wild flower buds striving to bloom
In the scorching heat of the harsh desert wind
Small colourful boats without a sail or a steer
Floating on sea, caught in a storm
Little chubby hands, not knowing what to hold
Grasp at whatever they can

My heart, it breaks
With a broken heart
I pray…from the deepest space in my soul
That space from which
A mother, deep in faith
Loves her child
That space from which
A mother, deep in faith
Cries for her lost child
That space from which

A mother, deep in faith
Strives to trust the will of God

I fall down on my knees
I bow my head upon the earth
I beg:

"Oh Merciful God!"

Let there be a safe haven
Preserve the sanctity of creation
The sacredness of innocence
The fragility of existence

Let there be a harbour for small boats
A shelter for blooming buds
Let little hands be given a finger to hold
Let Mother Earth give them nurturance
Please, let there be hope

Despite calamities that befall
Let grace find its way
In the darkest corners of the hardest hearts
Let love prevail
Let it melt away frozen tears of pain
Let there be a glimpse of light
In the blackness of night

Allow me to see your hand
In this intricate design
To perceive miracles
In moments of despair
My vision is blurred with tears
I cannot see
But I know there is a silver lining in the cloud.

## 82. Break Free

Chains of thought
Memories, wishes, desires
Imprison me
Ingrained scripts of what life is

Or rather what I think it's meant to be
Stubbornly strengthen their hold

Until I break into a million pieces
Or melt into a pool of blood
I will not be free

I will not be free
Until the chains
Have nothing left to hold

Slowly
Very slowly
Painfully
Bit by bit by bit
I feel myself breaking
Into tiny little pieces
I feel myself melting

I find myself Clinging

Then letting go
I sway

Between panic and deep calm
Between silence and a thousand screams
Echoing loudly in my head

From hope, to despair
Desperation to surrender

It will take its time
But the ball has begun to roll
I can feel the churning
The shift within
I will soon be free
Maybe destroyed
Only to come alive again
Deeper in faith
Stronger in spirit

Until that time
I tell myself -
Feel the pain
Be aware
Cry in agony if you must
Just don't forget to breathe
For breath is life
And life is truth
And truth is faith
And faith is freedom.

## 83. These days

These days
I often go inside myself
And stare at the dark spaces
Wondering
If there will ever be light

These days
I walk along the sea shore
Waiting for the waves to come
And wash the stains on my feet
The bruises on my soul

These days
I sit in the sun
Soaking up the warmth
Hoping that the cold numbness inside me
Will start to melt

These days
I look at the sky, feel the blues
Drops of molten heart
Slide down my cheeks
Like silent rain

These days
I curl up in my cocoon
Resting in faith

My broken wings need repair
I long to fly

These days
I realize
How much of a stranger
I've been to myself

These days
I face the mirror
Look into my eyes
Read the untold stories there
I find comfort in belonging to myself

These days
I sit in a corner
All alone
Wrap my arms around me tight

These days
I feel safe sometimes
And sometimes
Fear grips my bones so tight
I'm scared they might shatter

These days
I peel the layers that cover me
Search for pieces of my soul
That got scattered somewhere along the way
And try to see if they still fit

These days
I let the tears fall

Not knowing where they come from
Not caring where they go

These days I open heart
And lay it bare
In its wounded mess
Trusting Grace to come and heal.

## 84. Holding On

Frail
Like an old man of ninety two
The twig that hangs precariously from yonder tree
Reminds me of bonds that broke
And yet the twig
It does not break

One night, the stormy wind
It blew
The rain came down
The twig it broke

And when it fell onto the ground
I heard a sigh of agony
Was it the twig?
Was it the tree?
Was it the wind that blew it down?
Was it the ground it fell upon?

Was it just me?
Unable to let go.

# Short Poems

Leafless tree
No shade, no fruit
Only music in its bark
A flute waiting to be carved

A numbness wraps itself around me
I curl up inside it like a caterpillar in a cocoon
Not wanting to break free
Until I'm certain I have wings to fly

Enchanting forest
Sizzling fireflies
New-moon night
Studded with stars
The earth is in competition
With the skies.
Until the colour of blood

Stains the ink of words
Language will not do justice to real pain
So let's be quiet
Let's not reduce the breaking of the heart
To mere words

Sometimes, I just stare at the star-studded sky
And wait
As if the secrets of the universe
Will suddenly burst forth
And come to me
From the heavens above

Sitting alone
By the sea
I wonder
Why this salty wetness
On my cheeks

Like the drops of rain
Fall into the sea
And become the ocean
One inseparable from the other
In substance, heart and soul
That is how I loved you
That is the only way I knew

Stardust falls upon my window
Where last night the moon had come
The conversations I have
With the heavens
Are by far the best

How easy to forget
The fury of the tempest
When the seas are placid and calm

I trace with my right index finger
The lines on my left palm
These lines, they say
Contain stories of our lives

I trace with my finger
The lines on my palm
And feel you etched in me

Ray of sunshine
Enters a dark room
Illuminates cobwebs
Lights up one clean corner

Ray of hope
Enters a dark mind
Illuminates despair
Lights up one candle
Of faith

By being a drop in the ocean
You become the ocean itself
By being a part of creation
You become creation itself
Look inside you
See your soul
You will see it is part of a whole
You will see it is in essence divine
By being a part of the soul that's divine
You become the Divine itself

The absolute serenity
I have experienced
In rare moments of blissful peace
I wonder if it's the soul
Momentarily
Coming out from its abode
Pervading me,
Touching the layers that cover it
So that they slowly melt away

Tempests roar
Mountains move
The earth, it shakes and quivers
I stand on the edge of a jagged cliff
And say
"Thy will be done"

Bits of eternity
Lay scattered
Within this transience
And it is we
The people of the soul
Who have come to reclaim them

To be able to see
With the eyes of an innocent child
The heart of a passionate young woman
The mind of a wise old man
The soul of a seeker

Without the asking of questions
Without the seeking of answers
Sometimes we just need to be still

Here is the pain
From which my poetry comes
To you
It goes for healing

At the breaking of dawn
Light comes
So
At the breaking of heart

At times,
When I am in tune
With the frequency of the universe
I can feel it pulsating through my heartbeat
I can feel its magic in my bones

It is ever-so-subtle
This inner transformation
Attitude makes a dynamic shift
Actions only slightly change
What was before a simple handshake
Now becomes
Acknowledgment of soul

If you have nothing left, you have nothing left to lose
If there is darkness all around
Look for light within
When the road ends suddenly
Make your own path
Faith will walk with you

When life defeats you
Surrender to His will
When it throws victories at your feet
Bow down even more

Nothing quite renews my faith in humanity
Than the warm for-no-reason smile
Of a stranger as she passes me by
On the street

And is it anything other
Than the puzzling glory of God's creation
That in spite of not being able to see with their eyes
Blind people many times
Have a deeper insight into life

The belief that I can climb mountains
The knowing that I can shine
The joy that comes with feeling immeasurably blessed
Lies dormant within me
It is there somewhere
Waiting to be awakened

I sit and wonder during winter
If there will be another spring

The gurgle of the stream tells me
It's time to sing
Of times gone by
I may not be the one who drank
The cool spring water
But I drink the music of its symphony
As it flows away

In a hundred years from now
Perhaps,
You will be a small tree
In the forest
And I will be the flower
Growing in your shade

Show me the broken parts of you
I will kiss them first
Then gently put them in a small velvet box
The box I will keep very close to my heart
So that it feels the healing wholeness
Of unconditional love
Then, when the time comes
I will kiss them again and gently give them back to you
The parts will not be broken anymore

He holds my hand
I'm not afraid
Of falling
Anymore

Kisses my eyes
I'm not afraid
Of crying
Anymore

A bed of roses, velvet-soft petals
Fragrance that swells the air
Makes it a well of perfume
It is my heart, beloved
Let your soul rest upon it awhile
Sweet sleep, will find its way
To replenish your tired spirit

Nature talks to my spirit
The conversations happen outside the realm of my awareness
Yet somewhere
In a corner of my soul
Strings of music softly stir
A candle starts to burn

Oh beloved!
Won't you hold back a bit
From giving me such a measure of love
Lest, when I leave this earth and you
I find there is not love enough
In the heavens far above

My soul travels
To the edge of the universe and back
And through its journey
The only thing it finds worth living for
Is Love

I miss you
And yet how could I
You are so much in me all the time
When I wake up after a long night's sleep
It is you that I see
And when I close my eyes at dark
Your light is still with me

If you are in the wetness of my eyes
Then let my eyes be filled with tears
Stay with me in any form
Just stay

I see the horse
Gallop across
Open plains, boundless land
At the sight of freedom
My spirits soar

Could it be,
That when I think of you, you think of me
And in that moment
Somewhere in the realm of merging consciousness
Our thoughts meet and celebrate
Their togetherness

Let us be so intimate
So effortlessly close
One cannot tell, where I end and you begin

No beginning, no end
The story of our love
Weaves itself into the fabric of the infinite universe
And scatters itself into a billion stars

Share with me
The darkest reflections of your being
And I will look upon them lovingly
Till they lighten

Thousands of miles apart
Yet, nearer in spirit
Than two peas in a pod
You are so very close to me
I feel your breath in mine

By sweet serendipity
We chance upon each other
And soon, out of nowhere
Find ourselves immersed in something called Love

It leaves me drunk,
This passion with which you love
It leaves me convinced,
That there is heaven on earth

Let us go where stars abound
If black holes find us
We will become nothingness
Together

The sound of heavy breathing
The rapid beating of my heart
The soft crunching of leaves
As I walk the uphill trail
This symphony
Feels soothing to my soul

I threw away the silken scarf that you had gifted me
Alas!
Memories cannot be thrown away
So easily

Suddenly, out of the blue
The scent of jasmine fills the air
I wonder why, then realize
The memory of you passed by

Twilight zone
Neither light not darkness
Neither sun nor stars
Neither you nor me
Only faint traces,
Of our merging silhouettes

You gave me your presence,
I gave you my love
You gave me your promise,
I gave you my trust
You gave me the sky,
I gave you the stars
This give and take is heavenly

It's hard for me
And I'm not going to pretend it's easy
Just so that, the world does not have to see
A reflection of its own darkness

For you
I held wide-open the door of my heart
And as you stepped inside
My winter turned to spring

Deep silence
Broken only by the symphony of your footsteps
The lords of music serenade
A lover's secret escapade

Every thought of you,
Is a prayer for you

I'll show you my demons,
You show me yours
Together, we will embrace them
And watch ourselves transform

I discovered in you
All the treasures
I've been searching for

Loving heart
Gentle eyes
Healing touch
Beautiful soul

Anything less
Than real love
Is a consolation

Anything more
Than real love
Does not exist

We must feel intuitively
The perfectness of being
Like love,
It cannot be explained

For every seemingly wrong happening in my life
There are countless things happening right,
Waiting since forever
To be acknowledged

My hand is gripping tight although,
My heart, it wants to let you go
A tug of war between two parts of me
And I wonder who you're cheering on

Our very fist service to mankind:
The kind and loving thoughts we have
Towards ourselves and others

# *Testimonials*

"The reader of these deeply moving poems will get to know Arwa through their passion and sensitivity. The entire work has a uniqueness that reflects Arwa herself. I enjoyed it immensely."

- **Jonathan Bush** (Founder - J. Bush and Co.)

"The poems of Arwa Qutbuddin truly touch the heart and lighten the spirit; this book is a delight for the soul."

- **Huzaifa Khorakiwala** (CEO - Wockhardt Foundation)

To connect with the poet you can log onto
www.poeticsoul.in or write to arwa@poeticsoul.in
Thank you.

www.ingramcontent.com/pod-product-compliance
Lightning Source LLC
Chambersburg PA
CBHW070549050426
42450CB00011B/2786